① Look and speak. Colour and write.

desk

2 Look, read and write the numbers. UNIT 1

Put the book on your head. ☐   Turn around. ☐
Take off your socks. ☐   Jump down. ☐
Open the cupboard. ☐   Clap your hands. ☐
Put on your shoes. ☐   Wave the flag. ☐
Put the lolly in your mouth. ☐

2

1 Draw Conrad's super pizza.

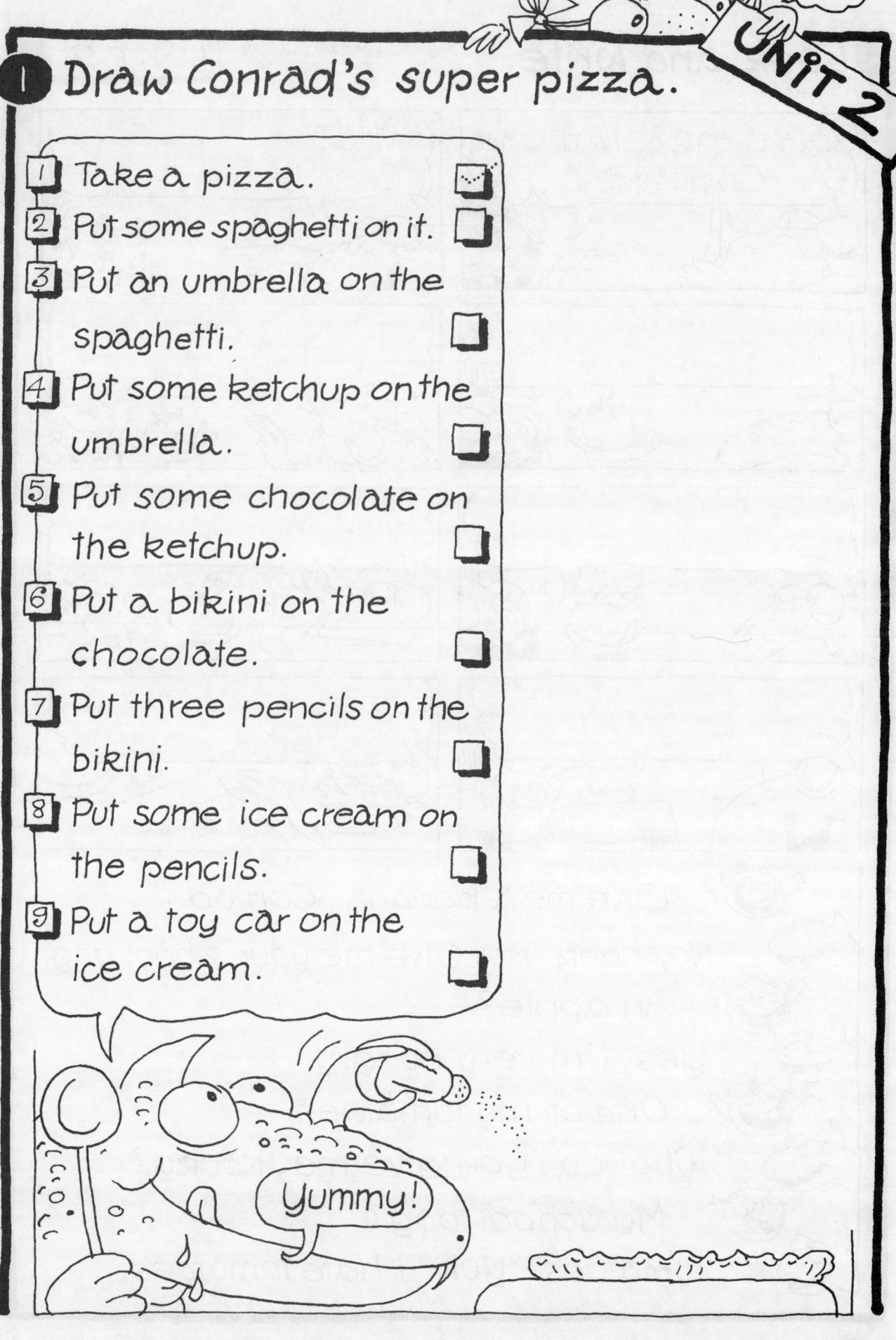

UNIT 2

Yuk!

1. Take a pizza.
2. Put some spaghetti on it.
3. Put an umbrella on the spaghetti.
4. Put some ketchup on the umbrella.
5. Put some chocolate on the ketchup.
6. Put a bikini on the chocolate.
7. Put three pencils on the bikini.
8. Put some ice cream on the pencils.
9. Put a toy car on the ice cream.

Yummy!

3

❷ Look and write. UNIT 2

"Give me a banana, Conrad."

"What"

Give me a banana, Conrad.
No, thank you. Give me your school bag.
An apple?
Yes, I'm very hungry.
One of my tomatoes.
What can you give me, Rocky?
My school bag?
Tomatoes? Yuk. I hate tomatoes.

4

UNIT 3

1 Look, read and put a ☑.

Put in some ketchup.

Drink from the pot.

Fly.

Take a big pot.

Go into the kitchen.

5

② Listen and put in order.

UNIT 3

3 Fill in the words.

UNIT 3

1. Archibald _takes_ a big pot.

2. He _____ a lot of things in the pot.

3. Archibald _____ out and drinks.

4. And he _____.

5. It's night. Archibald ___ scared.

6. He _____ from his pot.

7. Archibald comes down and _____.

is / drinks / takes / goes / flies / lands / puts

7

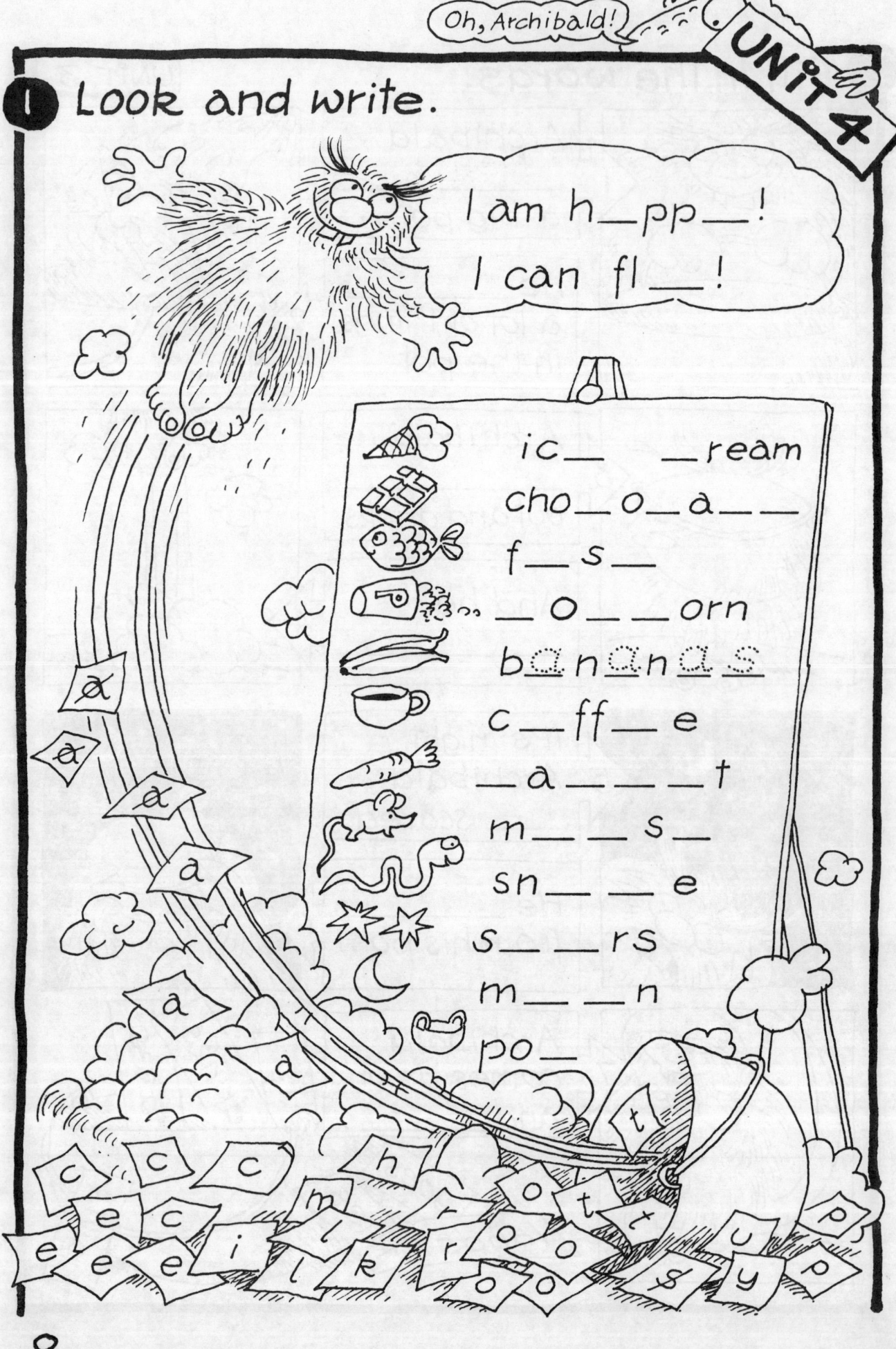

UNIT 4

1 Look and write.

Oh, Archibald!

I am h_pp_!
I can fl_!

ic_ _ream
cho_o_a_
f_s_
_o_ _orn
bananas
c_ff_e
_a_ _ _t
m_ _s_
sn_ _e
s_ _rs
m_ _n
po_

8

2 Write the story.   UNIT 4

Archibald is in the kitchen.
He takes a big 🫕 pot.
Abracadabra, cold and hot,
let's put 🍌 _____ in the 🫕 _____.
Abracadabra, cold and hot,
let's put 🍦 ___ ___ in the 🫕 _____.
Abracadabra, cold and hot,
_____ ___ coffee in the 🫕 _____.
_____ is flying.
It's night.
Archibald can see the 🌙 _____ and the _____.
It's very cold.
_____ drinks from his 🫕 _____.
Archibald falls down and lands.
He is 🙂 _____.
Abracadabra, wizzy woo.
I can ✈ _____ and so can you.

9

UNIT 5

1 Write the numbers.

_____   _____

_____   _____

2 Draw lines.

thirteen   fourteen   fifteen   sixteen
seventeen   eighteen   nineteen   twenty

70 13 17 80 60 14 30 19
      18 16 15 20 40 50 90

thirty forty fifty sixty seventy eighty
ninety

3 Read and write.

ninety minus sixty = thirty
forty plus fifty = _____
seventy minus ten = _____
twenty plus fifty = _____
eighty minus twenty = _____
thirty plus thirty = _____

UNIT 6

1 Look, write and draw.

Conrad & friends	Happy birthday, Tina. Here is your present.
	Hallo, Tina.
	Open it.
Tina	Oh, thank you. What is it?
	Lovely! A belt with five butterflies on it.
	Hallo, friends.

11

❷ Write a birthday poem.

UNIT 6

For my next birthday
please give me a book,
green sunglasses or a blue belt.
But please, don't give me chocolate.

For my next birthday
please give me _____,
_____ or _____.
But please, _____
_____.

12

UNIT 7

1 Look, read and put a ✓.

Your tooth hurts. ✓
Your head hurts. ☐

You make a bubble. ☐
You pull hard. ☐

You call your dad. ☐
Your face gets hot. ☐

You are angry. ☐
You are sad. ☐

You call your dad. ☐
You are scared. ☐

Your dad comes to help. ☐
Your dad is angry. ☐

He holds your head. ☐
He pulls hard. ☐

He calls the dentist. ☐
He pulls out your tooth. ☐

13

② Look and read. UNIT 7

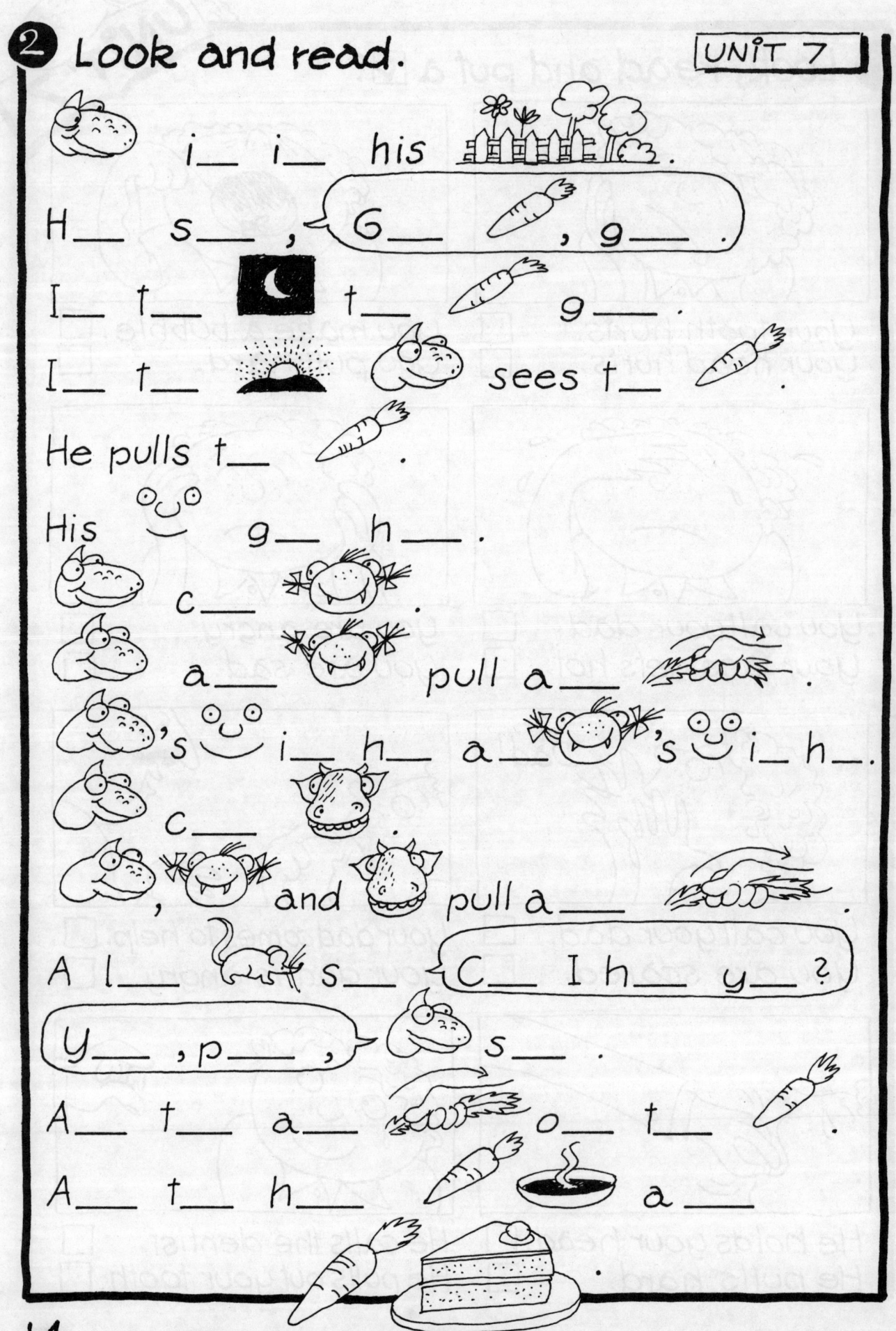

🐂 i_ i_ his 🌳 .

H__ s__ , G__ 🥕 , g__ .

I__ t__ 🌙 t__ 🥕 g__ .

I__ t__ ☀️ 🐂 sees t__ 🥕 .

He pulls t__ 🥕 .

His 😊 g__ h__ .

🐂 c__ 🐵 .

🐂 a__ 🐵 pull a__ 🥕 .

🐂's i_ h__ a__ 🐵's i_ h__ .

🐂 c__ 🐄 .

🐂 , 🐵 , and 🐄 pull a__ 🥕 .

A l__ 🐭 s__ , C__ I h__ y__ ?

Y__ , p__ , 🐂 s__ .

A__ t__ a__ 🥕 o__ t__ 🥕 .

A__ t__ h__ 🥕 🍲 a__ 🍰 .

UNIT 8

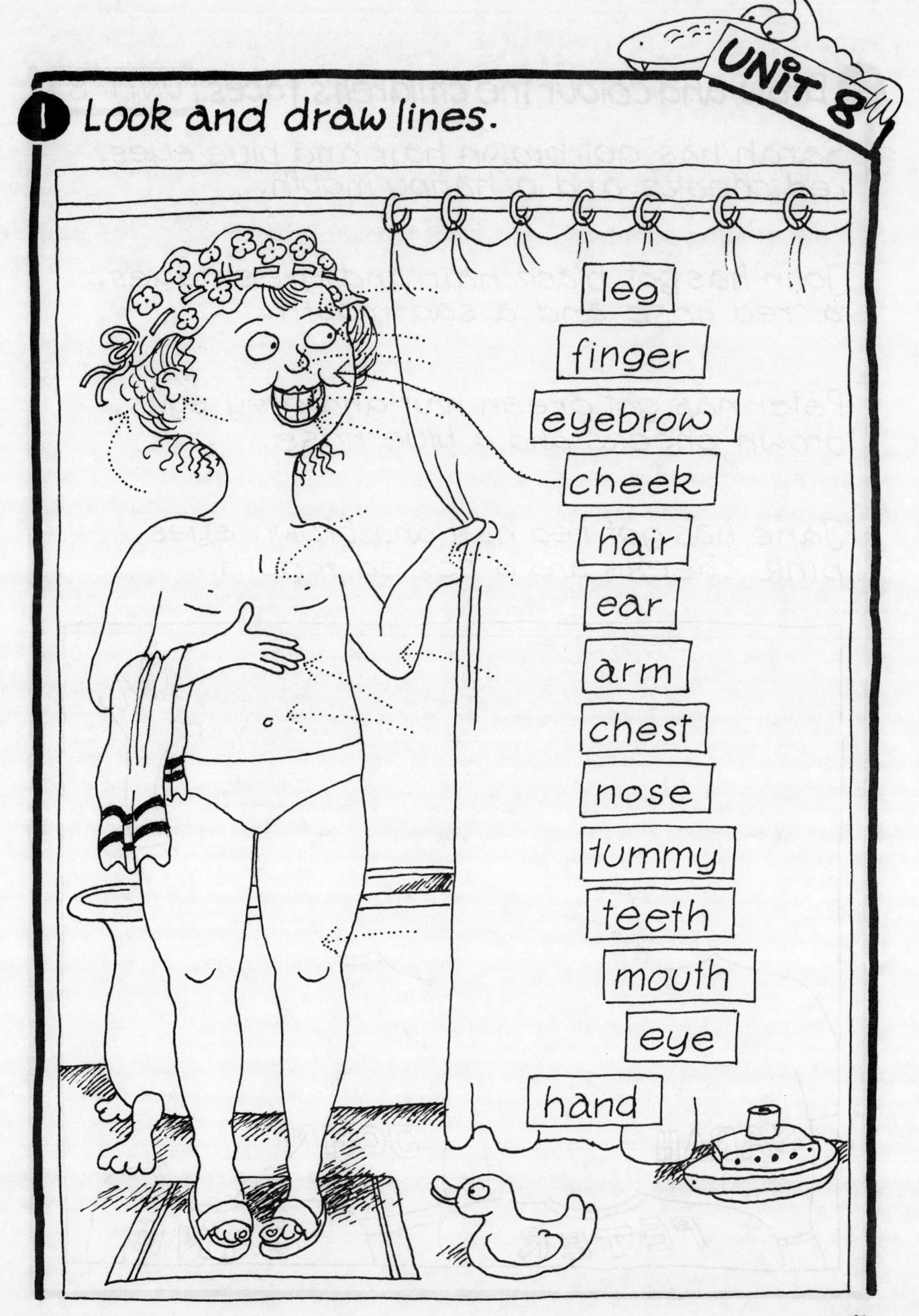

1 Look and draw lines.

leg
finger
eyebrow
cheek
hair
ear
arm
chest
nose
tummy
teeth
mouth
eye
hand

15

2 **Draw and colour the children's faces.** UNIT 8

Sarah has got brown hair and blue eyes, red cheeks and a happy mouth.

John has got black hair and green eyes, a red nose and a sad mouth.

Peter has got green hair and grey eyes, brown cheeks and a blue nose.

Jane has got red hair and brown eyes, pink cheeks and a scared mouth.

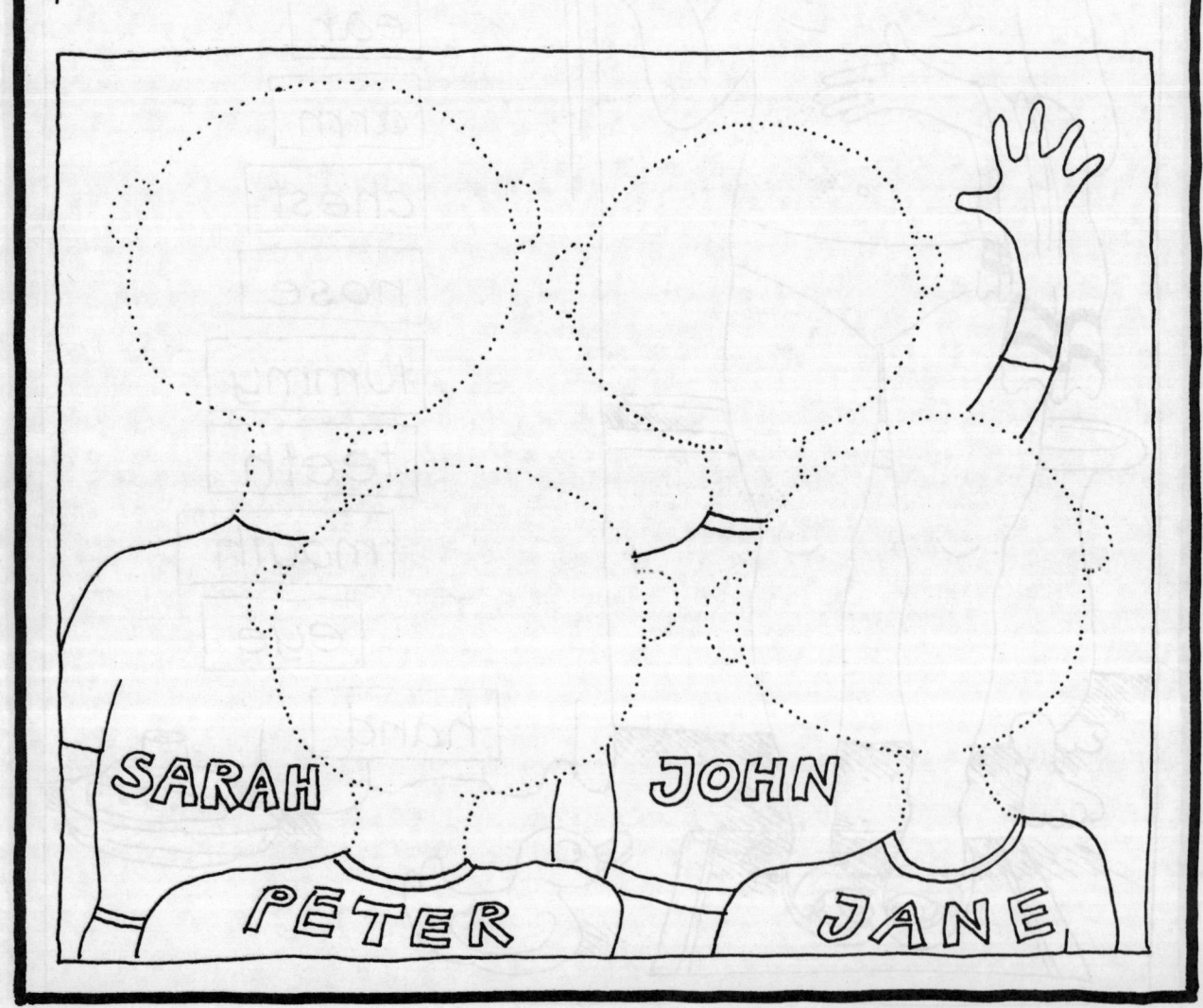

UNIT 9

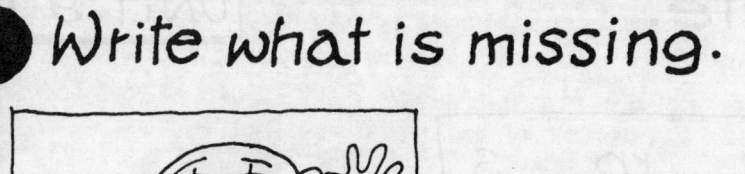

1 Write what is missing.

The clown's <u>right arm</u>, his <u>left leg</u> and his <u>hair</u>.

The teddy bear's _____, his _____ and his _____.

The doll's _____, her _____ and her _____.

right * hair * eye * ear * right * arm * mouth * right * leg * left * hand * left * foot * left * nose *

17

❷ Look and write.

UNIT 9

e_e_ro_s

ea_

h a i r (hair)

n_s_

e_e

t_e_h

c_ee_

m___th

c_es_

sh_u_de_

ar_

h___d

t_m_y

k_e_

l_g

t_es

1 Read, draw and colour.

Draw a long nose for Tommy and colour it red.
Draw a mouse on Ann's T-shirt and colour it blue.
Draw shoes for Mike and colour them green.
Draw sunglasses for Conrad and colour them pink.
Draw hair for Judy and colour it brown.
Draw an elephant on Pat's blouse and colour it yellow.
Draw a happy mouth for Judy and colour it red.
Draw an apple on Tommy's T-shirt and colour it green.
Draw a nose on Ann and colour it pink.
Draw jeans for Mike and colour them blue.
Draw socks for Conrad and colour them red and blue.
Draw ears for Pat and colour them orange.

UNIT 10

❷ Read and draw lines.

UNIT 10

He has got a long nose.

It is old.

He is happy.

He is old.

She is happy.

His hair is long.

She is old.

She has got a long nose.

He is sad.

He has got a snake on his T-shirt.

It is black.

Her hair is long.

She has got a snake on her T-shirt.

She is sad.

UNIT 11

1 Look and write the numbers.

☐ farm	☐ kitchen	☐ mountains
☐ school	☐ shop	☐ jungle
☐ swimming pool	☐ garden	☐ river

21

② Read and draw lines.

UNIT 11

Alice has a nice white dress and	says, "Ladies first."
She always says,	Alice, Oliver and Henry.
One day Alice	curly hair.
In the jungle Alice also	look at Alice.
Then the	me go."
They catch	tigers come.
Alice says, "Let	Alice first.
The tigers	"Ladies first."
And they eat	goes on a safari with Oliver and Henry.

22

UNIT 12

✳ Read and write the correct number.

one: snake ✳ two: elephant ✳ three: mountains ✳ four: jungle ✳ five: shop ✳ six: ice cream ✳ seven: tiger ✳ eight: mouse ✳ nine: swimming pool ✳ ten: curly hair ✳ eleven: river ✳ twelve: popcorn ✳ thirteen: white dress ✳ fourteen: safari ✳ fifteen: black dress ✳ sixteen: spaghetti ✳

UNIT 13

1 Look and write the numbers.

① glasses ② watch ③ belt ④ tights
⑤ socks ⑥ headband ⑦ sweater
⑧ sunglasses ⑨ skirt ⑩ shirt
⑪ trousers ⑫ shoes ⑬ slippers
⑭ T-shirt

24

❷ Look and write.

UNIT 13

socks

UNIT 14

1 Write what they say.

What's in your bag?

Oh, super. Thank you.
What's in your bag?
Put it on.
Yes, it's great.

Do you like it?
Here's one for you.
A headband.

26

❷ Read and draw lines.

UNIT 14

- Spaghetti?
- What's your name?
- Who's your best friend?
- What's in your bag?
- Do you like Tony?
- Is your T-shirt new?
- What's your telephone number?
- Happy birthday, Peter.
- Do you like my watch?
- How are you?

- Sandra. She is great.
- A new T-shirt.
- Yes, he's great.
- Yes, it's great.
- No, thank you. I'm not hungry.
- Yes, it is.
- I'm Sue.
- I'm fine.
- Thank you, Sandra.
- 3325.

27

UNIT 15

My hobby - eating chairs.

1 Write and draw.

playing football

camping ⦿ watching TV ⦿ listening to music ⦿ playing football ⦿ swimming ⦿ painting ⦿ playing table tennis ⦿ skating ⦿ skiing ⦿ collecting stamps ⦿ playing computer games ⦿

2 Write about yourself.   UNIT 15

😊 I like _____.
😠 I don't like _____.
😐 _____ is boring.
😃 _____ is great.

3 Read and write.

Let's play table tennis then.

I don't like TV. It's boring.

Let's watch TV.   Yes, fine.

29

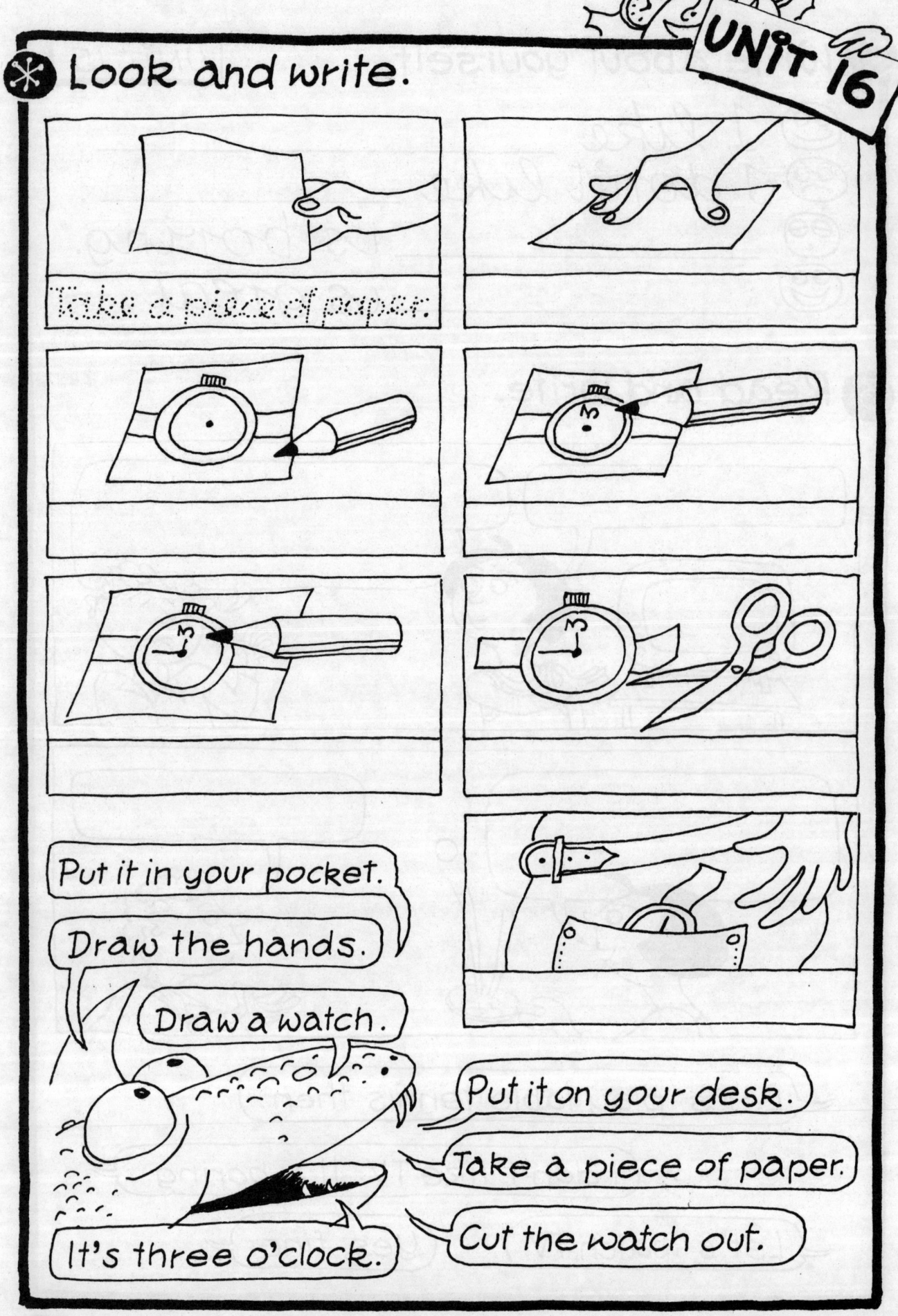

Look and write.

UNIT 16

Take a piece of paper.

Put it in your pocket.
Draw the hands.
Draw a watch.
It's three o'clock.
Put it on your desk.
Take a piece of paper.
Cut the watch out.

UNIT 17

1 Look and write.

drums

ms · gui · or · gan · re · cor
dru · tar · der · trum · pet

2 Write about yourself.

"I can't play the guitar."
"I can play the drums."

I can play the drums.
I _____ play _____.
I _____.
I _____.
I _____.

31

UNIT 18

1 Look and write.

It's a _____,
a _____
and a _____.

2 Look, read and write.

a bridge

a tree ■ a wood ■ a car ■ a monster ■
a house ■ a pot ■ a castle ■ a watch ■
a bridge ■ a hill ■ a monkey ■ a witch ■

32

3 Draw the pot of gold.

UNIT 18

1. Put it under the bridge.
2. Put it on the hill.
3. Put it under the big tree.
4. Put it in the river.
5. Put it on the elephant.
6. Put it in the farm house.

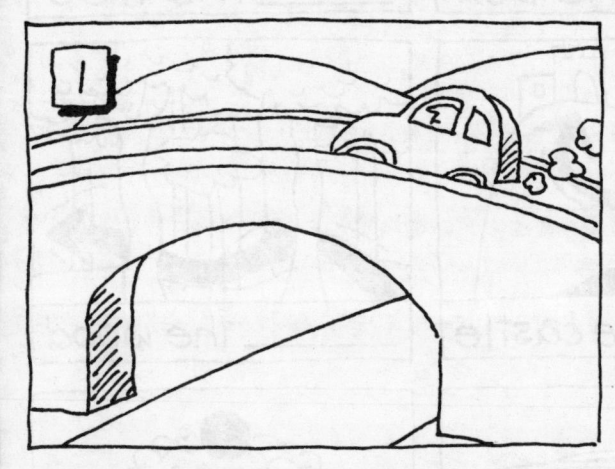

UNIT 19

1 Look and write.

- **up** the hill
- _____ the box
- _____ the tree
- _____ the bridge
- _____ the castle
- _____ the wood
- _____ the hill
- _____ the bridge
- _____ the tree

[letter tiles: on / through / under / in / around / across / to / down / up]

2 Look, write and colour.

I like the 🌙 _____,
the 🏰 _____ and the 🌳 _____.
I see the 🌙 _____,
the 🌙 _____ can't see me.

34

Read and mark the route on the map.

1. Don't walk under the bridge. Walk over the hill.
2. Don't go to the castle. Go to the old farmhouse.
3. Don't go with Rocky. Go with Emily.
4. Don't take the car. Take the bike.
5. Don't go to the school. Go to the restaurant.

② Look and write.

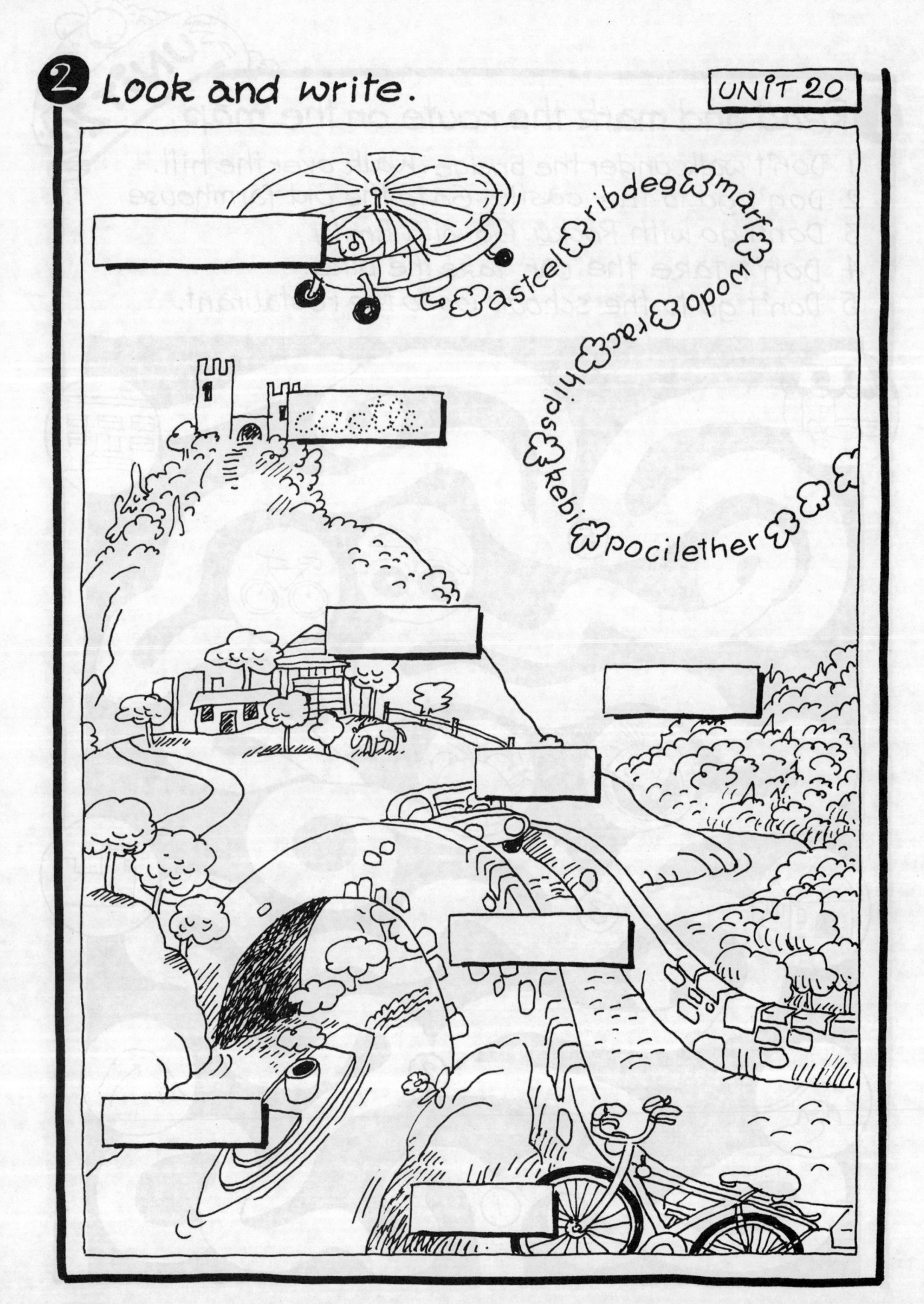

UNIT 20

astcel — castle
ribdeg —
marf —
wodo —
race —
hips —
kebi —
pocilether —

UNIT 21

1 Look and write.

cat

② Read and write the number of the sentence.

UNIT 21

☐ The farmer gives Jack some 💵 .
☐ The baker gives Jack a 🐱 .
☐ Silly Jack. No 💵, no 🐱, no 🌭 .
|1| Jack works for a 👨‍🌾 .
☐ The 🐱 runs away.
☐ A big 🐕 eats the 🌭 .
☐ Jack's mother is 😠 . She says:

(You must pull it along.)

☐ Jack puts the 🐱 in his pocket.
☐ Jack drops the 💵 into a 〰️ .
☐ Then Jack works for a 👨 .
☐ Jack's mother is 😠 . She says:

(You must put it in your pocket.)

☐ Jack pulls the 🌭 along
☐ Then Jack works for a 👩 .
☐ The 👨 gives Jack a 🌭 .

38

UNIT 22

1 Read and write the numbers.

☐ A pizza, please.
☐ OK. And to drink?
☐ The menu, please.
☐ Orange juice.
☐ The menu? Here you are.

2 Read and write.

Have some _____,

have some _steak_.

Have some _____,

have some _____.

Have some _____,

have some _____,

have some _____.

Don't be shy!

39

UNIT 23

1 Find the names of food.

X	S	Q	S	T	E	A	K	H	I
Y	A	B	A	N	A	N	A	S	G
C	U	E	N	S	J	K	L	C	R
H	S	A	D	P	M	N	O	H	A
I	A	N	W	A	P	Q	O	P	P
C	G	S	I	G	J	U	I	C	E
K	E	T	C	H	U	P	E	O	F
E	R	W	H	E	R	Z	T	L	R
N	V	F	D	T	U	V	W	A	U
T	O	M	A	T	O	E	S	T	I
E	F	G	P	I	Z	Z	A	E	T

2 Write the menu.

MENU

_____   _____

_____ soup

_____ soup   apple _____

_____   _____ juice

_____   _____

40

UNIT 24

1 Look and write.

Climb a tree.

Look happy.
Turn around.

Sing a song.
Look sad. Climb a tree.
Jump into the lake. Skip.

41

② Cross out the wrong words.

UNIT 24

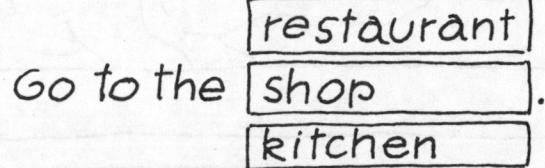

Go to the | restaurant / shop / kitchen |.

Buy some | orange juice / tomato soup / milk |.

Put it in the | pot / pocket / bag |.

| Fly / Walk / Swim | home.

42

✱ Read and draw.

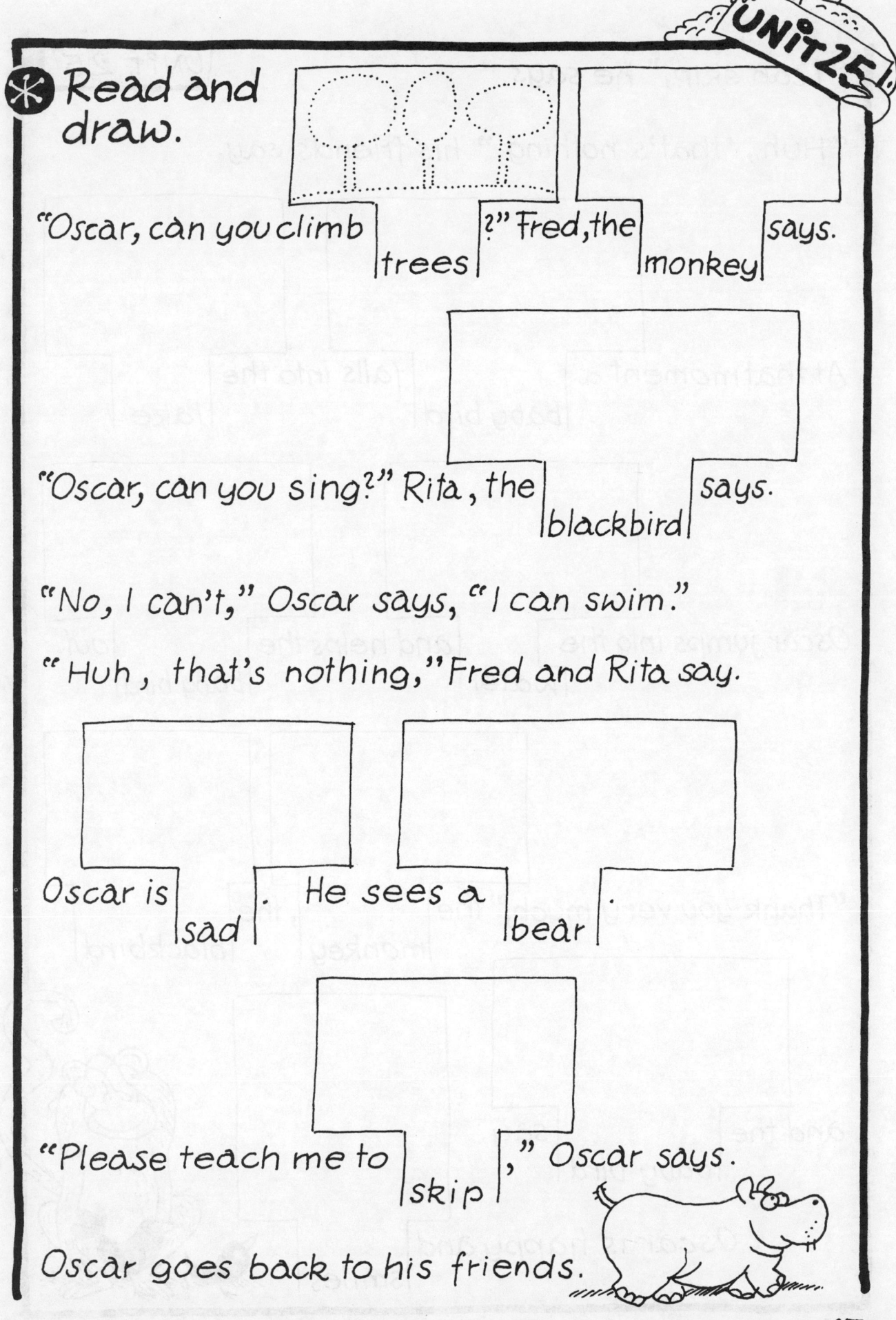

"Oscar, can you climb trees?" Fred, the monkey says.

"Oscar, can you sing?" Rita, the blackbird says.

"No, I can't," Oscar says, "I can swim."

"Huh, that's nothing," Fred and Rita say.

Oscar is sad. He sees a bear.

"Please teach me to skip," Oscar says.

Oscar goes back to his friends.

UNIT 25

43

UNIT 25

"I can skip," he says.

"Huh, that's nothing," his friends say.

At that moment a baby bird falls into the lake.

Oscar jumps into the water and helps the baby bird out.

"Thank you very much," the monkey, the blackbird and the baby bird say.

Oscar is happy and smiles.

44

UNIT 26

1 Look and write.

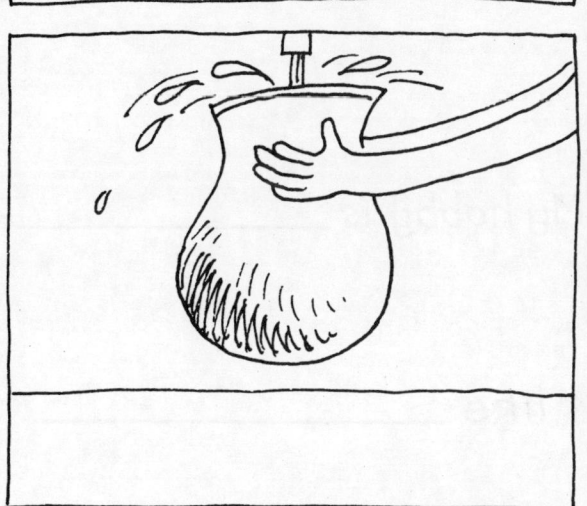

Go into

Drop it on the floor. | Go into the garden. | Cry.
Put water into it. | Take a vase. | Pick some flowers.

45

2 Complete the sentences. UNIT 26

This is me

My name is _____ .

I'm a _____ .

girl • boy • green monster

My hobby is _____ .

swimming • playing football • watching TV • listening to pop music • playing tennis • skiing

I like _____ .

I hate _____ .

chocolate • popcorn • coke • chewing gum • ketchup • ice cream • hamburgers • sandwiches • pizza • lollies

I'm often _____ .

I'm never _____ .

happy • sleepy • scared • angry • hungry • tired • sad

My favourite animal is

the _____ .

butterfly • crocodile • tiger • frog • elephant • cat • flamingo • horse • mouse • monkey • dog • snake • hippo • bear

1 Look and write.

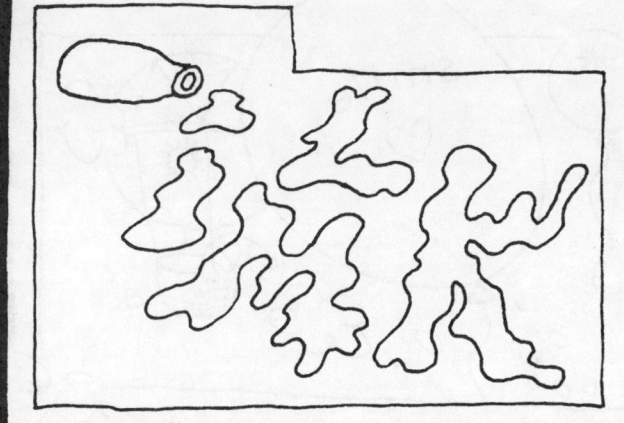

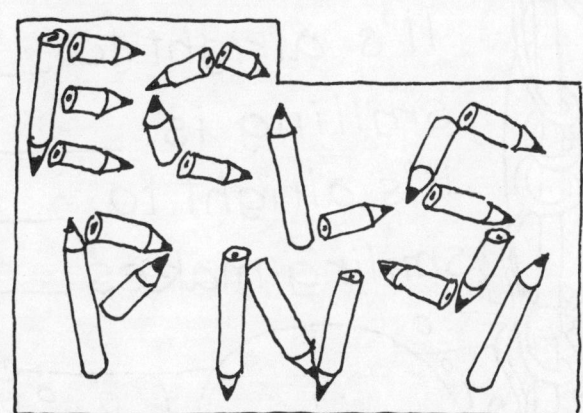

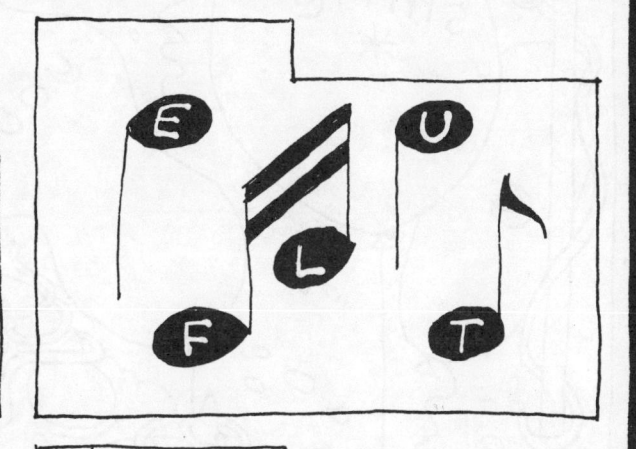

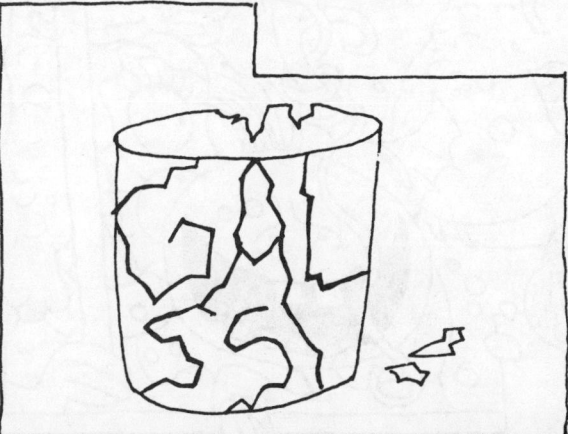

2 Write the words and colour the balloons. UNIT 27

It's alright to _____,
smiling is _____,
it's alright to _____,
smiling makes ____ feel ____.

better
smile
smile
you
okay

* red
☾ blue
♤ green
☼ yellow
♥ pink

48